Falling in Love with Fellow Prisoners

POEMS

Gwendolyn Zepeda

with Preface by Lucha Corpi

Arte Público Press
Houston, Texas

Falling in Love with Fellow Prisoners: Poems is made possible through a grant from the City of Houston through the Houston Arts Alliance.

Recovering the past, creating the future

Arte Público Press
University of Houston
4902 Gulf Fwy, Rm 100
Houston, Texas 77204-2004

Cover photo by Jackson Myers
Cover design by Ashley Hess

Zepeda, Gwendolyn.
[Poems. Selections]
Falling in love with fellow prisoners : poems / by Gwendolyn Zepeda.
p. cm.
ISBN 978-1-55885-769-8 (alk. paper)
I. Title.
PS3626.E46A6 2013
811'.6—dc23

2013021733
CIP

∞ The paper used in this publication meets the requirements of the American National Standard for Information Sciences—Permanence of Paper for Printed Library Materials, ANSI Z39.48-1984.

Printed in the United States of America

13 14 15 16 17 18 19 10 9 8 7 6 5 4 3 2 1

Contents

Falling in Love with Fellow Prisoners

Ain't I a Woman

Strongly Felt Sensations

Preface

Many years ago, a friend who loved talking on the phone called me. She was contemplating penning a collection of personal stories. After recounting in detail how her day had been, she asked: "How would you know you're a writer? How can anyone tell?" I answered her query with one of my own: "When you feel the urgency to express a strong emotion, or you're so bored with routine you can't stand it anymore, do you reach for pen and, paper or the phone?" Silence, then a click at the other end, and I knew our conversation—and possibly our friendship—was over.

My response must have given my friend something to consider. Perhaps it also helped her to harness the will to respond to the urgency not by talking but by sitting down often enough to get the writing done. A few years later her memoir saw the light of day.

I was reminded of that conversation as I listened to award-winning fiction writer, children's book author and poet, Gwendolyn Zepeda, in conversation with radio host Eric Ladau in April 2013. Zepeda spoke candidly about her life as a trailer park mother, whose way of staving off boredom was watching TV or surfing the Internet. Soon, she joined a group of bloggers who exchanged online comments on TV programs. She became a popular blogger, which led to her landing a paying job as one. In fact, she became the first professional Latina online blogger.

In April 2013, Zepeda was named Houston's Poet Laureate. She is not only the first city laureate, but also the first

Latina to receive that well-deserved recognition for her work. When Ladau asked about the things that inspire her to write poems, Zepeda replied, "Usually, they are about anything that evokes strong emotions in me. Something will make me feel angry, nostalgic, joyful or sad, and I will quickly write a poem on my smart phone. I used to carry a note pad, but now it's much easier to use my phone."

Zepeda added that walking across a parking lot that day, she had seen a baby wearing a pair of skinny jeans. She reached for her smart phone and wrote a couple of lines about the stylish infant.

I was delighted with her comments. I will probably not own a smart phone or an electronic pad soon, but I have always carried a small notebook and a pencil tucked in a pocket of my handbag. In every room in my house, there is notepad and pencil handy at all times. Although I gave up the idea for safety reasons, long ago I also had a small recorder taped to the dashboard of my parrot-green VW bug to use during long road trips.

For the poet, the task of writing down a line or an entire poem as it occurs is not only wise, it is vital. Whether the poem is lyrical or narrative, love or epic, philosophical or imagistic, with consonant or assonant rhyme, structured as a sonnet, ode, elegy, haiku or blank verse, one thing is certain: the poet must be receptive to the poem the moment it comes. Poetry is elusive. It requires that we acknowledge the many disparate elements that come together to form the poem and record them by any means at hand when they occur to us.

Many times, the lines of a poem appear suddenly, fast and furious, like a meteor shower. Just as quickly they burn and dissolve in the poet's subconscious. If the poet captures them as they begin their luminous trek, they become the seeds that fall into imagination's fertile ground and take root. Then the poet nips, waters and shapes it until the poem has nothing more or less than all essentials for its survival. What happens to the poem after it becomes a separate and complete entity is a matter of deliberate choice for the poet.

Naturally, we are inclined yet afraid to show our work to perfect strangers, who may not appreciate it. I have been approached by younger poets, who are seeking publication of their first poetry collection and want my advice. I don't discourage them from sending it out to various publishers. But I always point out that making one's work "public," and becoming a respected poet begins long before one publishes an entire book of poetry. Poetry is meant to be heard as much as read on the page. The best way to get one's poetry known is to read it to an audience as often as possible. Among the listeners, there might be magazine or periodical editors, or a publisher, who might develop an interest and ask the poet for a submission. Nowadays, social media provide good opportunities for poets to have their work circulate widely.

Gwendolyn Zepeda has been writing poetry since she was a child. Publication of her first major poetry collection comes as the culmination of many years of writing poetry, of making her poems known to a variety of audiences and readerships at public readings, in periodicals and magazines, online publications and several chapbooks.

Zepeda's collection title, *Falling in Love with Fellow Prisoners,* hooked and reeled me in immediately. The mere phrase "falling in love" evokes a violent, uncontrollable drop down to a place from which escape may be nearly impossible. In fact, love is often described as a tender or sweet trap. Falling in love is diving into the well of unfulfilled desire, where satisfaction and joy in love as in life are hard to realize. The experienced lovers, "the fellow prisoners," know all this and hope for the best, or plot imaginary escapes. The younger lovers suspect or sense the danger involved, but intrigued by love's promise of pleasure, they are willing to risk the pain and take the plunge. Zepeda writes:

> The inward face
> that holds itself blank
> is begging to suffer in love. (29)

Zepeda's poetic voice is unsentimental, essential and definitely urban. Her unerring vision scans the urban landscape and discovers the many prisons along the way: a "bomb shelter" where two lovers wait for a nuclear holocaust; the store window, where a "Baby Doll" sits "poised, bored tease in / a building that gleams"; a bathroom stall where Eula, a delusional spirit, endlessly retells her story; the American Dream home; a car, speeding down an open road to a fortress, the workplace.

With polished, precise and direct lines, the poet's eye bores through the drab, concrete walls of the workplace to expose the stark, monotonous reality behind them.

> The walls are beige, the carpet's dark beige, all the metal and / fake wood are beige and brown. The prints on the walls / are beige. And brown. And taupe. And gray. And gray-ish, brownish purple. (21)

In this prison, inmates have jobs to do, but "no one cares" what they do or if they do it "well" or "cheerfully . . . or with any feeling / whatsoever, or not." People trapped inside it endure the monotony of days in quiet desperation, when "boredom" is "almost as bad as loneliness" (21). All anyone wants is:

> to see the
> sun glint and feel
> the swim motion forward. (35)

Or create an imagined escape, as watching through a window,

> A medium-sized Black Bird flies over the grass and the fountains. / To the vine-y-webbed bayou that's right there for both of us— / for him and for me—to be wild in. (16)

But when finally someone escapes and gets home, she is "too tired to do a god- / damned thing." And all she has left is her imagination, her dreams:

> . . . All drama, all violence, all sexy, fast
> fast fast and so very interesting, all night long. (21)

At home or at work, hope is a caged animal, like the kitten or cat at an animal shelter, waiting for someone to take him home, or the mynah bird outside a dry cleaners, "Shiny and black with his face / orange and gold," who mimics a passer's-by "I love you" (75). But it is also a full term fetus at the moment of birth, and a mother's first dream wish for him or her:

> we cut the strings, and fully formed,
> you float away. I shade my eyes and
> watch. I wish you ever higher. (49)

The imprisoned human heart, the spirit, longs for freedom. But escape from prison, even when possible, demands constant effort, daily payments in sweat and blood, with the balance due paid in tears. Every day, Zepeda tenders a poem for that freedom.

It is my hope that the fashionable infant in skinny jeans will find the work where she belongs, so I may enjoy reading the poem, as I have enjoyed reading the poems in *Falling in Love with Fellow Prisoners. Enhorabuena,* Gwendolyn Zepeda. Encore!

Lucha Corpi
Oakland, California
July 2013

For Dat, with love

Raised Catholic

A Locust a Hundred Feet Up

Is watching me through his
monster eye
head like a gar holding
fairy wings
He wants to fly into
my hair
He wants to fly into
my head
and skitter it with
chitinous things
He wants to lay the
farmers bare
He wants to eat
'til Armageddon
Sent by God to teach a
lesson
Remind me of my
sin
skittering under skin
I shiver under ugly eyes
And then he flies
away

Paranoid

The paper skin lady with faint gray whiskers
who simmered rice pudding did say
that I should have had my tail removed upon Baptismal Day.
I felt the bump far down my back, did not know what to say.

I dreamed the Devil made a mark on my banana bread.
when I was thin, the men all 'round would call me pig instead.
Now that I'm fat and strangers grind against me, nothing's said.

Roaches used to crawl above my head upon the wall.
I knew that God had sent them, messengers winged and small.
His wish to see me dead required no reasoning at all.

When the woman on the news said Satan often told her things
I smiled to find another who might know my hidden parts.
I never told my therapist about these secret dreams.
She thought that I was good. I didn't want to break her heart.

The Mexican in Me

makes me superstitious. Makes me respect my elders for fear that, otherwise, my grandmother will fly down from heaven to slap my face. Makes me talk really loud when I'm excited or mad. Makes me get mad whenever I feel like it, like it's a perfectly healthy thing. Makes my butt big. Makes my lips big. Makes my eyes big. Makes me pale green in certain lights. Makes me want to wear shiny, pretty things. Makes me love babies and animals. Keeps me from getting my ass kicked. Makes me mean, but only because I love you. Puts moles on my skin.

(Makes me diabetic, some day soon, maybe. That's what put my grandma in heaven, along with other things.)

It makes you accuse me of using this half to get by, which I'll ignore.

It makes me a little bit magic.

The White in Me

makes me love elves and dwarves. Makes me want to hang cross-stitched samplers in my house, with letters and glyphs that mean things. Makes me have a 401(k). Makes it okay for me to wear nothing shiny, sometimes. Lets me think I'm so smart at school, even while I might be stupid at home. Makes the cops listen to my side of the story. Makes you trust me at garage sales. Gives me stretch marks and makes me burn in the sun. Makes me sweet to strangers, even when I want to hate them.

It makes you accuse me of using this half to get by, which I'll ignore.

And that makes me a little bit magic.

Tempt

There is a demon-eyed girl.
God, don't let me wish that
I could eat her
could feel her shiny sin inside.

I wish I was a bat-winged
girl in hell, sometimes, so I
could more appropriately
enjoy this.

Prayer to a Man

God is our father and I'm Daddy's girl
get whatever I want
but all I've got the guts to want
is getting through the day

Heavenly Father, Heavenly King
I bypass the mother
what does she know
she's good for flowers, she's good for foot pain
I don't pray to some woman in aluminum foil halos
saw her reflection in a rose-crusted clock
ninety-nine cent store
butterfly-slopping blanket on the wall
laminated holographic prayer card
milked by The Son, hey, lady, get a job
I don't see your name in no Big Three.

Our Father who art in Heaven
should I sit on your lap
laugh at your jokes
whisper in your ear "job, house, clothes"
probably let you kiss my cheek
and giggle "your whiskers tickle!"
Now can I get my presents and go?

Father of men, holy be Thy name
Maker of the world-goes-round
Do I have to swallow my pride or what?
Do you want me down on my knees?
Do you want my face wet, am I pretty in pain,

should I moan out the words "oh God, oh my God . . .
can I please just get through your world tonight safe
to my tired and groveling home?"

It's pretty You-damned sad getting to the point
where I say: Let's strike a deal.
Just keep my kids safe
I don't care about myself
an eye, tooth or nail, take whatever you want
keep them safe from the ones that you made in your
image, please
handsome god
heavenly father
holy king
righteous warrior
shining quarterback
sacred cowboy
special man

Elders

And what are you?
You're jealousy.
You're hate, old lady.
Hatred.
Old man, you're bitterness
personified.
When your kind dies
this world will be
rinsed clean
except for your seeds.

These People

On the news there's people in the Valley getting arrested for leaving their children in hot, locked cars. It was a hundred and three yesterday. Grandpa walked through Wal-Mart unhindered. The kids were okay. They were hardy.

In my life there's people I know who only criticize their loved ones. Shitty bitchy words just tumble on out of their mouths. Their parents did the same to them. To make them hardy. Made them hard.

The lady on the news says there's a phone application that helps you remember to think of your kids. Download it now.

The lady on the news says there's a teacher who won an award. This teacher is at your daughter's school. She seeks to undo all the lessons you teach her.

I Had a Job I Hated

A Man Needs a Woman

A man needs a woman even if he's strong.
A woman to help and support and admire him.
A man needs a woman to be there beside him.
Even when he's much more
powerful than you.

Sometimes a man needs a shoulder to
whine on.
Sometimes he might need a
wife on the side.
Sometimes a man just needs
someone to blame
or a thing to think thoughts of when
he's feeling small.
A potential container for all his
small thoughts and feelings and
bodily fluids.

He'll let you know and you'll be there to
do it.
And if you can
type fast
then that's even better.

They told me that when
I applied for the job.
I needed the money so I said
okay.

I Ruined My Work Shirt with Jack in the Box Taco Sauce

How are we living if
our nutrients corrode us.
How are we living when
one dot of brown
makes a difference in how
we're perceived.

Strongly Felt Sensations of This Morning

The parking garage is a video game. It takes skill to apply just the right press of pressure to the gas and the brake. To swirl up and up, reflexively avoiding the beat-down pedestrians, the unseeing SUVs failing to yield. The big Robot Bass throbbing hard in your ears as you kick this game's ass and collect your high score. Wait, there isn't one. Oh, well.

Outside it's beautiful and green. If you don't like warm Marches—warm Februaries, Januaries, then get out of Houston. Don't complain anymore. While you're whining your mantra, "I miss snow! I miss seasons! I miss Kansas, too, Toto!" I'm silently thanking my gods for the warmth. Thank you, Sun. Thank you, Spring. Thank you, God. Thanks, Equator. Thank you, Sweet Plastic Jesus with paint-chipping smile, under the Christmas trees, here where it's warm in December.

But I get beat down as I walk inside, to the cold, beige womb of a money-grubbing mother. The deeper I go, the more the walls filter the sunlight to dusk. To spore-ridden nothing, asbestos-y substances burning my lenses. Bleaching and leeching the everything out of my face.

Will lipstick help? No. Will a coffee break help? No. Will Monster.com help? No, not so far.

A gift comes: the privilege to carry some paper far, far down the hall to the world of my betters. And then! I linger in their doorways. I'm using their windows to look at the Sky. I joke with myself in my mind about running and crashing right through them, no, not to fall all the way down to my death or to rescue.

Oh, no. But to shake off the glass shards and then fly away. A medium-sized Black Bird flies over the grass and the fountains. To the vine-y-webbed bayou that's right there for both of us—for him and for me—to be wild in. It's holding the trees that will hold me so tight when I sing. Oh, wait for me, please. I'll be free for you later, at 4:45.

No matter what happens inside the beige walls, it can't make me stop loving Spring. And I strongly suspect that Spring loves me right back. So there, take that, Beast of Money, Cold Hell.

The Elevator's Tight Squeeze

The smell of hate or tied-up
something burns the dregs
and smolders. Hard-forced
Air vibes push from
you to me. Your
chemistry is broken,
Sir. Your tie/shirt/money clip/
pedigree do not
obscure your scent.

Like a Baby Doll

Blank-faced I sit in this
window. Pretend not to see
the men spraying and sweating
outside, that they're looking
at me.

Or else I'll watch over their
work like a mami, will
pantomime questions or fear
for their safety. The rough ropes
look brittle, the rusty hooks
liable to break.

But most days I pretend not to see
them while they pretend that they
don't ever see me. (At least un-
til they peek.) (I see them when
I peek.)

I pose, poised, bored tease in
a building that gleams.

The Homeowner

Drive back and forth
a rush-hour tide
I strive to regain that feeling I felt
when I thought that this was worth it.
The drive is gray.
I cry. I think of everything we've gained. Paint chips and
blonde and white children and clippings
and trash days and swimming pools and
girls on the Pill, fresh-faced and vacant
not girls on the corners with babies
in wombs in their swollen tight jeans.
No, that stuff's far away now. We live
in a paradise of our own making.
We're making a living and paying our
taxes, becoming Republicans up by
our bootstraps and living the good life
now, living the fucking American
Dream. So why am I crying. It's
just that the drive is so gray and
the faces insipid. The tide is receding
but never can rest and I'm driving for
ever. I'm driving toward something
I sure can't complain about, something my
parents could never have had so it makes them so happy
to see me like this now, driving
and driving and wipe away tears now. I'm
laughing because it's so dumb. The whole
thing's so laughable, isn't it?
I put on some music.
It helps.

In the Parking Garage

This morning, I wanted to interrupt her
fierce concrete stomp.
Look into her auto-pilot eyes and say,
"Did you know you're the prettiest?
the prettiest girl in the building?"

As if my approbation is a prize
better than catcallers
down on the street.
I wish she was only a flower or a
shell on the beach.
I'd look silently. Still now, I do.

If ugly words stopped flowers' blooming, would
you say all your best words to bloom them again?
And does that make you selfish?
If flowers could hear, would they need us
to point out their power?

A Bad Feeling

Something almost as bad as loneliness is boredom. Especially boredom you can't escape.

The walls are beige, the carpet's dark beige, all the metal and fake wood are beige and brown. The prints on the walls are beige. And brown. And taupe. And gray. And gray-ish, brown-ish purple.

This, after the expensive repainting and re-carpeting and general renovation. This was what they came up with.

I know my job but no one cares. It really doesn't even matter if I do it well or not. Or if I do it quickly or not. Or if I do it cheerfully, or distractedly, or hatefully, or with any feeling whatsoever, or not.

There's nothing else to do. Nowhere to escape to except into more nothing-colors and nothing-ness. Go drink some coffee if you want. It'll only keep your eyes open bigger when there's nothing to see. Go joke in the hallway with people who feel the same but can't admit it. You're caught under water with them all, and nobody's going to yell for help.

Count the minutes—count the fucking milliseconds—until you go home. When you get home, you're too tired to do a goddamned thing.

Your dreams are all colored. All drama, all violence, all sexy, fast fast fast and so very interesting, all night long.

Eula in the Bathroom Stall

I've got to go
and so I make my way
into the stall
but find I'm not alone.
I hear a groan
and know she's there.

It's Eula there
who makes that groan
and oh, I wish I were alone
inside my stall
because she's way
into her story, started long ago.

Her monologue goes
on, no matter who is sitting there.
She tells the way
her breasts have grown
so swollen, or her ovaries have stalled.
She says her family's left her all alone.

And if she were alone
she'd still be talking, just the same. She'd go
on for hours, no shame at all.
And yet I'm pinned there
by her words. I groan.
I cannot get away.

I want to get away
because I need to be alone.

I've grown
aloof in my old age. I go
insane when Eula's there.
She has no shame at all.

I'm an animal
in Africa. I feel the way
they do, so vulnerable, crouched there
silently listening for all the lions who'd love to suck
my bones
'til Eula goes
and makes a scene with jumping, shrieking, plumage,
groans.

So we have grown
like animals, we hide in stalls and silently go
insane with vulnerability. Ashamed, afraid, we
crouch there all alone.

Unless loud Eula awaits us,
inside her bathroom stall.

9-to-5, After Noon

Under glassed-out hot sun
you're boil-in-a-bag
or sinking your head to
plywood stone.
Nothing here is handsome
and you're crowded but alone.

No one here can hear it
the pressurized bore-hate
that holds us taut.
And you're caught up high
in the catbird seat.
Or your stick in that window.
Looked at, boiling hot,
alone.

His Son Is His Everything

His son's always hungry and he lives through
his son's appetites. A flint's struck in
his eyes as he tells me, inserts into
my head the images that must rock
his body to sleep. A deer's head
nailed to the wall, glassy-eyed, sniffs at
the filmy pink panties adorning its
horn, its antler, I mean. "A trophy
on a trophy!" he tells me his son said.
He says with a head shake, pretending
chagrin. He describes the pink-panty
girl who beat on his front door and
cried, and he tries not to snigger.
Next comes a vision of anonymous
Muslims sweating and running in fear
at the sight of the particular insignia
emblazoned upon his son's breast.
He sweats, himself, maybe, telling the
vision of brown men beat up in the
hot bloody desert.
So proud.

I feel a bit dizzy at my desk now.
There's too many bodily fluids
especially testosterone and bile.
I see his stories, his smile, and smell
the fear. My own. I'm afraid of his
son. Of his laughter. Of the fact that
my whole life depends
on satisfying this man's needs. I'm

afraid for my spawn to get mixed
up with his spawn because my
own son is my everything. He's the
only reason I'm here now this
afternoon listening to this man piss
into my brain.

His son is his everything. His son is
the sum of his rutting and antler
butting. His son is his reason for standing
here, telling me what to do.

Falling in Love with Fellow Prisoners

Words for Nerds

The sexiest men
are the sexless men.
I want to wake them up.

The inward face
that holds itself blank
is begging to suffer in love.

If you're secretly a warlock
don't feel guilty, it's just fine.
If you're secretly a monster
then I think you should be mine.

Unrequited

I like it when I'm loved, she says
but can't love in return.
That feature got burnt out
she said, but go ahead, I'll
let you love me, first.
Okay, he said. Of course.

Zombie Maker

He knows you're the kind of girl
to throw his love away.
But he still loves you so, and he
says it all on his guitar and he's
on stage so sad, and all of the
other girls listen and
sway.

But you look away and laugh.
And I look at you and say,
come to me now, oh come to me,
you wicked girl. You
vicious thing.

Blondes, More Fun

Gold girl run
on through my head
One day I'll be
your winner.

You may never see
it's me here
striving struggling
hoping
You may never see
it's me
fighting monsters
for you.

Or you may see and
still not care.
You're just a pretty face.
There's nothing behind
your face when I
see it in my head.

Be Witch

What are you doing? I
like to picture you in
five shiny leaves that
make a flower on your ear,
frolicking in the woods,
a messenger bag full of
fairy dust or a
cobbler on the stove,
a quieting baby on the
hip and pine trees in the
window. A black cat on
the window sill and
either way, your spells
are all unbroken. Your
magic's all in working
order, potions in the
cupboard. Bubbling's
on the fire. A twinkle
in my breast imagines that
you might be happy.

The Flower for December Is Narcissus

The weather outside was frightening and I wore out
  my welcome when I
locked you inside and made you hold up
constant mirrors of me.

Don't act cold. I need your face to
face my fire and warm me. Or go ahead and say
goodbye. I'll find myself another man to thaw.

Fishing

The dysfunctional conversation
over, he says: Let me let
you off the hook
now. Let me cut you loose.
He laughs.
Isn't that funny, he
gives her permission to
go?
She thinks it's funny to
imagine herself as a fish
that he catches each day.
A wish that she grants him. He
whispers: Be mean to me,
please.
She does, it's granted. She says:
you're welcome and please don't
go fishing tomorrow.
Not the same hooked wish, the
snare kiss that's tangled in
nets and wet spangles and bitter
like brine
that draws her, catches her
again and again, when
all she wants is to see the
sun glint and feel
the swim motion forward.

Freckles

Freckles on my fingertips
like fairy dust
or when you touch
a butterfly
except it dies
and you're alive
and you exist
and here you are.
I touch your skin.
Your freckles won't
come off but I
enjoy the thought of
making you
more naked than
you are right now
with me.

This may be your favorite song, but

you're mad because I sang the words wrong.
Don't you see?
The man said hiding place, his voice so brusk
and fakely British.
I heard honey glaze, my voice so free and
plain and confident
A honey glaze was the lyric needed in the
song that played while we rode that street.
We ride in a sugar maze. The man who's singing
doesn't know that you plus me is sweet amaze.
How could he have known while recording what
he thought he had to say? That we would be
inside a personal honey glaze today?
His love was like a hiding place, it's
not my fault that he was sad
and couldn't understand.

(The Suess Carried Over)

His eyes shine black
His skin is gold
He has a part
I like to hold
And when I hold
that part within
Bang! Bang!
We rush and
rush again.
His form is warm
within the fold.
Our eyes see black
and red and gold.
And now the moment
has been told.

Our Love Is Like a Bomb Shelter, Baby

I like lying safe with you
here in the dark, but still
keep planning in case
I'm left alone.

Why do I hide the bright
jars of pears away,
bring out the dusty sardine tins and
force us to chew the bones
over and over again?

Checking myself for signs of
mutation. So tired of
running from mushroom clouds
that my metaphors
don't make sense.

He dialed me by accident and I eavesdropped

Tiny phone in my hand, tiny time machine,
bringing me love from last night.
Listening to nothing for well on ten minutes. Imagining
him late in his car last night. Starry Houston flashed
by out the windows. He changed the CD. This one
had a slow, quiet intro. I listened. He burped a small
burp. Then he spit out the window. The sounds were
disgusting but also endeared as they taught me
his normal restraint on these points.

Ain't I a Woman

Hush Now

You called it unspeakable horror,
the things this girl went through.
But when this girl grows big and ripe
she'll be the one to tell it.
She'll have a whole hell of a
tale to tell.

And you won't be able to speak
when you hear it.
But that doesn't make it unspeakable.

It's just not spoken by you.
It's not your tale to tell.

Girlfriend

When are you going to call me
When are you going to show me
When are you going to prove me
Wrong

When will your phone call complete me
When are you going to take turns and
Be me
When do I give up and set myself free

Embarrassing to Admit

Give me an apron and rolling pin,
I want to gently scold you.
A mother and wife I'd surely be.
Give over to me and see
how well I'd play the lady parts
assigned while on my knees.
And working that power, all
dusted with flour.

My grandmother said when
the day was through, if the
dishes were dirty and her
face unmade, she knew to do
the lipstick first, before
her man got home.
The rest would follow.

Let me tell you what to do
with supplication and honey-
skinned turkeys. A voice
like a whip. Hot oven, red
lips. Yes, let me be your
mommy-wife until I'm bored
again.

Situational Anemia

My body decided to waste a bunch of blood cells and iron on a baby that never came into existence, and now I'm freezing to death.

Also, more than the freezing and the aching and the cranking, I feel vulnerable today. Like an orphan in the snow and like sharks can smell my blood.

I have this marled old-lady sweater that keeps me sort of warm. I wonder if people realize that I'm also using it to shield my person and the thin feminine fabrics that are the only other barrier between them and me.

Instead of the sweater, I wish I had a leather parka lined with wolverine fur. Instead of a barrette, I wish I had a helmet with spikes, and then steel wire wrapped around me like cotton in a protective, noise-blocking wad.

For good measure, I'd hang a sign that says "Leave me alone. Or violence."

I went and got some green tea. That should help, but I'm starting to think that the only real cure will be getting out of here and lying in the sun for a while. In a plain old bathing suit (and a tampon).

Nicked Spine

The anesthesiologist
drives back to the
hospital. Sirens full
blown in his head. They said:
When her head's
lying low, then the patient
is smiling but if her
head's lifted to
forty degrees, the
patient face fills with pain.

This means danger
lawsuits, paralysis?
Taking a hit, hard,
to his med mal.
Cursing the woman
he runs a red light
remembers last night
the way that she
flailed, and he
nicked her spine
and he bit his
tongue hard at her
whining.
Why don't they stay still.

The anesthesiologist
drives back,
fast as platelets.
He knows how to
fix it:

Blood snatch!
Spine patch!
Blot, clot, caught!
A simple
procedure like it should
have been last night.

Now in her womb
oops her room
bright white nurses fawn.
The cries of the
spawn while the
mother lies smiling
as long as her
head stays down
not lifted up more
than forty degrees.
"A simple procedure,"
he explains and
admonishes
"But only if you can
keep still."

The mother kept
low on the bed there
just laughs at
him. Laughs like
he's nothing or
making a joke.
"Everything's simple,"
she tells them all
"Now. Remember, I
gave birth last night?"

Child

I made this. Within my blood
a chemistry swirled that
created everything inside you.
Like a seed you came out small, but
contained it all. Some for
now, most for later. Like a
balloon. The kind you make
yourself, with liquefied plastic and the
air you breathe. I breathed you out, you steadily
rounded out, just like a soft, slick globe
still warm from me. I pushed
and blew and sighed and hoped until,
the circle done, you entered space,
we cut the strings, and fully formed,
you float away. I shade my eyes and
watch. I wish you ever higher.

Self-Acceptance

I wanted to be an Aphrodite, but it turns out I'm Hera instead. I walk through the playground and little kids I don't even know slide over toward my legs, like flesh magnets, my big hips their umbrella. Stray cats see me and meow for scraps. Dumb dogs lick my hands.

If you know me in real life, you know I'm followed by a single word, repeated over and over. "Mom. Mom. Mom." It's pronounced at slight length, with a crescendo and then a decrescendo. It fades in and out like a siren. Two sirens. Three.

Hera has a stern face. "Get over here now," she demands. "Stop that fighting," and "Come fold this laundry—what am I, the freaking maid?" and "Hold on. I'm in the bathroom."

But you remain by her side because she will never let you go hungry. No matter how late your supplications, she will create your science project supplies in time. She will catch your vomit, of course, in her hands and hope to kill anyone who tries to hurt you.

Sometimes Hera longs to venture from her hearth for a moment—to go to a movie or maybe to a bar. She glares at Aphrodite on the television screen. Sighs and flips through a magazine. Skims through a story about some pervert turning a girl into a swan, a lute or a linden tree. Checks again to make sure the door is locked.

Then Hera yawns and falls asleep against her throw pillows that smell like the shoes of little boys.

Malady, Adjusted

Pretty plump wife
your brains are clogged
have I got a product for you.

That's a pretty plush life
you've got going on
so why're you feeling blue.

If I was to take and
flip your life
dump you out cold in the
middle of the night
what would you do?
Now what in the whole wild world
are you going to do?

Proposal

I'm ready to be my own bride
and lie in my wedding dress in my own bed.
I'll lock the rest of the world outside.

It won't be you at my side.
It won't be Jesus, it won't be the sea.
I'm ready to be my own bride.

Once married, there's no need to hide
myself from my spouse, there's no need for shame.
I'll lock the rest of the world outside.

I gave myself a merry ride
but the chase is finally over.
I'm ready to be my own bride.
I used to feel lonely inside
but I figured out the cure for that.
I'll lock the rest of the world outside.

The day has come and I swell with pride.
I've finally captured the girl I deserve.
I'm ready to be my own bride.
I'll lock the rest of the world outside.

Omega Wolf

I was climbing, on my way to achieve a summit
a fame, a fortune, a promotion with a fifteen percent raise
When you stopped me. You said
hey, what're you doing I see
your boobies your booty your
big jiggle sugar thighs!

I was shining, standing on the stage
accepting accolades, face arranged into
modesty and grace. And when
I stepped down you
caused me to pause, saying
hi there, girlie girl I see you looking
good there I don't like so much such a big butt but
if you'd let me I'd pork a pie girl and you can
be in my magazine!

I've been catcalled and
I've been harassed.
But this wasn't that.

I was running on a track or I was
power walking a mall.
You impeded me.
For one tenth of a second, sidled your
way into the corner of my eye. Mouthed
hi, look at me now whatchoo doing whatchoo
know that I can think about your vagina!

Omega Wolf, I see you. You're
working yourself up. Would you
fling seed toward me, hope for it to
stick to any part I've left exposed
to burrow, gain purchase and
make for you a child who can
climb, who can shine and who
outrun you?

Strongly Felt Sensations

That Music Made Me Cry

She says she doesn't feel it.
At first I think she's lying
and why? It's such a strange,
bald treachery.

Her face says no, and now I
believe it, and now I look
away, as if from a hot
pink stump, a burnt stiff
smile.

At the Animal Shelter, Was a Volunteer

She showed me sick kittens in cubes
that had holes like dots on dice
made for stacking and about to be
stacked in a room that would
filled up with gas, with a
big garage door facing
out to a dumpster convenient for
emptying boxes.

Boxes and boxes that stack and stack.
Kittens without end who are there and then gone.

In order to deal with the memory
I have to consider them surplus.
Too many animals and not enough
demand. Like snack food gone
stale, like shoes out of style.
I told her I went there to shop and
she showed me a holocaust.
So much for customer service, I thought.

While I hate to remember, I tell everybody I
know. They say I'm dramatic and tend to
exaggerate. I tell them to hurry and
get to the shelter before it's
too late. Save the kittens!

I went for one kitten and left with two cats.
(The older ones' shelf lives are shorter and
I picked two ripe ones about to expire.) She

boxed them in cardboard with holes in a pattern like dominoes. Gave me an unhappy smile. Walked me to government employees and bid me goodbye.

After Hours of *Girls Gone Wild*

my retinas are embossed by
lumps of nubbly flesh, hard
pressed against my TV screen.
Thousands of members got
stoked then stroked, I'm sure,
in response, and it's the same
beige, pink-tipped, poky flesh.
And my retinas crave some
mental zest—something a
little bit more like sex.

Curtainless Bohemian Girl

Everyone can see, except
for why
Watch the boys who
watch you, or maybe
write a poem or
two
Maybe ride your bike to
someplace new
A soundtrack rises 'round
There's nothing better to
be doing
'Til you're old and
vulnerable
and cover your
windows.

Sunflower

The title of this poem is Sunflower.
I liked the sound of the word.
Sunflowers stared from the side of the road.
Their faces were lovely and so was the word.

Why There Are So Many Songs About DJs

The marionette Master
reaches inside and
changes my heart rate.
Makes my blood flow, warmly
sting, buzzes my head 'til I
can't feel a thing except
for what he gives me.
Makes his force reverberate
and I don't mind a thing.
Make my body scream and
if you're good I'll be a zombie
for you. Reach inside me, wring
me out and late at night
I'll feel you in me, I'll feel
wrung like after all the
long days at the beach.
Your wavelengths rock me back
and forth now, even in my sleep.
And if you're good you'll string me
up and along until I drop. If
you're good I feel the strings of
sound that go between.
Betwixt your spinning and my
heart. Feels like love.
Please don't stop.

Winter

I like pine sap. Who doesn't like to sit
still for a while and take note of the turn
of the world. Our earth is a green and brown mystery,
and your boss lets you stay home to notice for once.
Once in November, once in December.

I like stories of rags to riches. I love
stories of rags to incredible God-like power.
The idea that angels will herald a hitherto
under-appreciated soul. The heavens themselves will
set down a big star. That whole drama appeals to me.
Plus it has donkeys and sheep. All
set to the drum of the sweet Baby's shadow, that
rags-to-remixed drummer boy.

I like sugar and I like sparkling. Red berries, candles,
hot rum or wine. Buzz in my ears of the trusty
old harmonies. Handel and hand-bells. Donnie, Marie.
Suck on the pulp then and lick up the juice.
Ignore the pith, the seeds, the rind that's
the rest of our lives.

This Girl I Know

She cries "I'm broken!"
And calls down around us
all the predators on land, in sky.
I don't know how to mend her.
She screams like a bird in my ear.
I turn my head. The smell
of blood is making me sway.
I turn and slip away. I've
had my fill. I'm in the water
where it's warm and deep and
she can't follow.
Goodbye. Good luck.

Springtime Is an Indomitable Monster

They iced the azaleas down today
dropping bits of winter in vain
tried to rain on the springtime parade
that should have come two weeks later,
on schedule for the yuppies.
And yet

the neon blood spewed forth. They
grew fully grown. Spring sprang,
sprung to life right under their
dirty fingers. It told them,
"You will never, you will never."

Spring lets you bed it, not
bend it. Not bend to your will.
You won't. It will.

Diner Trick

His voice slides low beneath the
clattering.
His shoulders rise, too, with a
sigh.
We hold our breaths but can't be still.
We wait for his announcement.

"I didn't want to have to do this, but . . . —"

Out come the Camels.
He tamps on the pack.
Out comes the lighter.
It glows the tip orange.

And then, 'round the corner,
here comes our waitress.
All laden with burgers.
Our father has summoned her
up like a genie.
She lays down our plates and he
stubs out his cigarette.
We cheer.

I believed he had magic.
I believe it sometimes still.

Live Band

I loved that girl when she
played and twanged in
banged-up blue jeans
twirled her lips and
smoked a pack of nothing
but especially when she
sang my dream.

Traveling

I missed your telepathy because I'd missed the tail end of a TV tragedy. I called you this morning. You'd watched the same story but picked up right where I'd left off. You described a character played by Jeremy Irons. You told me the twist that I'd missed. You completed my thought train and I missed you.

I'm waiting at the airport for a plane that will carry me home. You'll be waiting at the Kiss & Fly or the Park & Bye or whatever cutesy name they call it.

Earlier I talked about funerals with strangers. I joked about us joking, in our interdependence, about our own deaths. I said that we'd argued, fought about who would go first. "Not you. Don't leave me." They laughed at my anecdote.

But I'd had to cut it short because my chest hurt. I made it a joke when I
knocked
on
wood
made the sign of the cross and touched my hand to my lips. The only serious prayer I ever do.

Whenever we're apart I miss you. When we're gone for too long, I lose touch of your thought train, get
scared of a time
if
when
God
the only thing left would be missing you.

Drive Through

cherries in the mouth
cooked against a sizzled
crust and reddening 'gainst
my teeth, in greasy lust
they tell me that this sort
of thing is bad
but i don't mind as long
as it gets hidden in my car
along with everything the
way i play the same songs
never stopping and it's
an old song you wouldn't
approve.

i'm driving very far
so fast along the
highway that nobody
else can see my face
right through the glass
so clearly so invisibly
the glass a safeguard in
its own clear-see-right-
through ability. the glass
in candor and its truth
hides everything about
me. maybe you see
my smile as i drive by
but you can't think of

why before i'm gone
i'm gone goodbye i'm
hidden and i don't
have to hide.
goodbye i smile.

A Link

With her, I lay on the bed Sunday mornings watching TV
Marilyn Monroe in black and white
kung fu movies packed with shirtless men
stretched, supine, safe on a king-sized surface of
sturdy polyester, nylon-stitched and muted floral print.

With me, you sit up in bed on a Sunday night
we watch dance competitions and
wannabe celebrities with dignity for sale.
I hope you feel the same as me with her.
Safe on embroidered microfiber and loved.

You Are Missed, Mr. Rogers

One day I turned on the TV because I was
scared to start thinking alone.
I turned it on to hear the noise but saw you
there instead. You said "How long is a minute?"
And I thought of a lot of
funny, mean answers. And then you said
"Let's see." You put an hourglass on the
table. The tiny kind filled with bright white
sand. And I scoffed.

The hourglass showed us just how long a minute
was. And a minute was just long enough to
make my heart slow down.
The only thing in the background was the
railroad whistles and jazz. I thought of
nothing. I only listened until the
minute was done. You said that you'd
be back when the day was new, and I was glad.

Until the other day. Or I guess it's been five or
six years since you died. And I'm
thinking about you and crying again but it's
not because I'm sad. These tears are part of that
good thing you told me. You gave me your
minute; it's still here whenever I need it. And I
remember what you said. It's such a good
feeling to know that we're alive.

Vietnamese Noodle House

Saturday mornings
the concrete glows humid
or else sleek gray, in the rain.
We enter fluorescence and
everyone stares but I'm
used to it. Over in the corner
in the coin-filled shrine
the Buddha got apples today.

Our regular waitress
has a beautiful face
long hair tucked under a baseball
cap. If I try to say the words:
Pho! Tai! Lon!
She laughs. She smiles. She's
proud of her pupil.
When my boyfriend says
"Three, please," she frowns.
"Americanized bastard," maybe she whispers.
The standards are higher for him here, we know,
but he's Chinese, not Vietnamese.
Chinese, not Vietnamese.
Oh, well.

Number Eleven is a soup with raw beef.
the soup cooks the meat for
you. Stir it and watch.
The food on my plate now is vinegar, sweet.
Vinegar, then sweet
with soda and limes.

Outside, the dry cleaner's bird
gets some sun.
He's shiny and black with his face
orange and gold.
"I love you!" we tell him.
"I love you!" he says. Then he
screams really loud, something
in his own language.
Then whispers sweet something
in Vietnamese.

I love him, I love you, I love
pho tai lon.
The concrete glows humid
or glistens in rain.

Also by Gwendolyn Zepeda

Better with You Here

Houston, We Have a Problem

Lone Star Legend

To the Last Man I Slept with and All the Jerks Just Like Him